Poetry *e*-motions

Poetry *e*-motions

By:

Stephanie A. Galloway-Callaham

&

Other works contributed by:
Wanda A. Wheeler-Alford

www.bookstandpublishing.com

Published by
Bookstand Publishing
Morgan Hill, CA 95037
3868_4

Copyright © 2013 by
Stephanie A. Galloway-Callaham & Wanda A. Wheeler-Alford
All rights reserved. No part of this publication may be reproduced or transmitted in any form or by any means, electronic or mechanical, including photocopy, recording, or any information storage and retrieval system, without permission in writing from the copyright owner.

ISBN 978-1-61863-502-0

Printed in the United States of America

Dedication

This book is dedicated to any and everyone that has lost a loved one, had a broken heart, been betrayed or manipulated due to falling in love. For the ones that have loved too much or not enough. For those that took love for granted or thought they were in love but were only in SEX. For those mistaken puppy love for real love. Especially for those that are still in love with someone that is not theirs to love.

Forward

My past shouldn't be able to hold me back.
My present shouldn't be able to hold me down.
My future will always be there waiting for me.

S.A.G-C

I'm not full of shyness, just full of awkwardness, of not knowing my self worth and others ignorance is what kept from doing things that are important to me. Yet, I have to start somewhere.

S.A.G-C

Table of Contents

God's Plan	1
Often	3
You Were There	4
I knew	5
What is Love	6
Beloved	7
Season's Change	8
Heartfelt	9
I'm a Big Kid	10
Searching	11
To My Child	12
Away	13
Love, or Is It?	14
Have I Ever Told You That I Love You	15
I Never Understand	16
True Story	17
Torn Between The Two	18
Why I Love So Much	19
Why???	20
Truth	21
Looking at You	22
I Hate to See you Leave	23
Creation	24
You	25
Which You Have	26
Incomplete	27
My Best Friend	28
Xo's Lullaby	29
I	30
Look Deeper	31

Times....Oh Times	32
No One Ever Knows	33
Broken Heart	34
Anything	35
Light to Dark	36
My Way	37
Employee of The Month	38
Breaking Time	39
Hater in My Camp	40
What's Inside	41
The Past, The Present, The Future	42
Remembering	43
My Promise	44
In Me	45
One World	46
What About Feeling?	47
Invisible Love	48
Outside	49
Looking	50
Peaceful-(for grandma)	51
My Solemn Prayer	52
A Better Way	53
Misery	54
Come Back to Me	55
What Do I Do	56
Mistaken Identity	57
Going On	58
This Love	59
Imagination	60

A New Beginning	61
Gone, but Not Forgotten	62
Giving Heart	63
Please, No More	64
Lost Soul	65
I Hate What I Know	66
Self-Judgement	67
?	68
What's Next?	69
Reality of it All	70
Lost	71

God's Plan

Once upon a time, a long time ago a star was born. She was brought down from heaven prematurely and with a disability. The humans told her mom that she may not make it and to take her home to be around loved ones.
But, God had other plans.
The Little Star was stranger than anyone has ever seen and lived longer than expected. The humans tried to correct the Little Stars disability with several attempts, they made her days easier to bare, but announced that she will never walk.
But, God had other plans.
More surgeries were done and the humans said that she will never be able to feel. God had other plans. Then one day a vision appeared to the star and it was a familiar face.
Nothing was said but all was understood and after that night her pains were all gone, but her suffering will remain.
Yet, God had other plans.
Little star was raped at gun point. Jesus said my father has sent me here to protect you just close your eyes and it will be over soon. I'll hold your hand and get you home safe and she did. Little Star was told during her last year of high school that she couldn't go to college. After completion God made sure the same woman was there to see his work, Cause, God had other plans.
She even continued to get her Master's.
Little Star wished she had someone to love her for her. Jesus guided her to the path that God had planted for her. Little star was told that she could never bear a child, but God had other plans.
Little Star has accomplished a lot in her life and still plans to more. This is just a story to let everyone know that when times seem rough and your plate seems full. Jesus is

walking you through it, and God has it all planned. Little Star is now a Super Nova and the world can see her brightness, of course she has haters, why she will never understand, but God understands and is always smiling at her and sending angels her way.

Often

You often said you loved me. I often wonder was it true.
Because it's hard to believe you love me
When you constantly do the things you do.
You kiss me on my neck and whisper sweet things in my ear.
I'm disappointed to find you are not near.
And then you make good love to me promising me you'll never leave,
but as soon as the thrill is over. You give me all the more reason to grieve.
I hear you say you love me, but I feel you hurting me much more.
I often wonder did you love me or is it was just a line to score.
So, if you ever truly loved me, please come forth and tell me so.
Because I often wonder if you meant it but I'd rather you let me know

You Were There

You were there when I wore mom out and you never screamed nor shout.
You made me laugh at your silly faces and took me to all of those wonderful places.
You changed my diaper when I made a stink. Mom looked at me and gave a wink.
I'm glad you're here to watch me grow you're the coolest guy I know
You held my hand and watched me sleep. You were always there when I would weep.
So, on this day I would like to say
Happy Father's Day.

I Knew

The first time that you kissed me, I knew.
The first time that I felt your touch, I knew.
The first time that I saw your beautiful face, I knew.
The first time that you held me forever, I knew.
The first time that you said I love you, I knew.
I knew then and I know now that you're my mommy
So, I'm here to say thank you, and Happy Mother's Day..

What is Love

Love is a feeling that's stronger than any other nothing could ever take its place.
Love is constantly thinking of the one you want not wanting to allow them any space.
Love is to desire something so bad your heart feels it as much as you.
Love is going to any extreme for someone no matter what you have to do
Love is thinking of someone else more than you think of yourself.
Love is dreaming of them at night not wanting to dream of anything else.
Love is calling just to hear their voice or even just to say hi.
Love is giving them the benefit of the doubt when you know what they say is a lie.
Love is trusting, wanting, and needing them unconditionally.
    You will never understand love, never in eternity.

Beloved

Ask me not why do I love thee because, the answer is yet to be found.
I can't explain why I love thee so but I just feel that we are bound.
Yet, I love thee more than life which means I'll give my all to he, the one I loved all yesteryear, I shall continue loving for eternity.
What giveth the day of light to withhold this feelings so dear to me?
Only the sight, the thought, and the love for my eternal, beloved he.

Season's Change

The Season's changing as you see and I'll enjoy it with my family.
Last year we were apart and now we're together which will make this year even better.
No more long distance calls or train trips to New York.
I'll no longer have to ride the bus in the dark.
My family is together once and for all were finally together during this beautiful fall.

Heartfelt

I'm sorry for all the pain and discomfort that I brought to you. If anything there is I am capable of doing.
I am certainly willing to do. I know we're still new, with so much to learn, yet, I'm open to each new idea. Whatever I can offer to make things right, I promise you, I will give My thoughts are with you, also is my heart, I'm feeling you completely. Your sadness tends to be my pain and I accept that, but apologize deeply. For any hurt issue you may face, I always will be here. Through morning, evening, day or night-- with you, I share the tears. I accept your heart on this given day, just as you've accepted mine. I'm here throughout the thick and thin; here during each minute in time. If ever you need me, you know where I am, only a phone call away. Once again "sweetness", I apologize for the pain I've caused on this day.

I'm A Big Kid

I'm a big kid now, so I've been told.
What they really mean is that I'm getting old.
So, I'm off to kindergarten to learn new things.
So, watch me soar and spread my wings. So, goodbye for now to my old friends.
I hope our friendship never ends.
Wish me luck as I do you, maybe I'll make a friend or two.
Saying goodbye is never easy to do. You've taught me so much and I want to say thank you.
I'm moving on to another start but please remember you're in my heart.
I'm taking with me the love that you share.
It really showed me how much you care.
So, thanks a lot for all you've done you'll always be my number one.

Searching

Looking hard in search of a better day.
Constantly wondering if the Lord will ever look my way.
It can't possibly continue to be this way forever.
There has to be some light; my life has to get better.
What will I do if ever it doesn't?
Is it God's will, that my life mustn't?
I wonder what he has in store for me. What possibilities, what achievements, what many opportunities?
The harder I search the more disappointed I am.
To find no better way, just another jam.
Please, grant me something so I can see the purpose of this life you have given to me.

To My Child

I wanted to die, I wanted to cry. I wanted to leave it all behind.
But when I look at you, you keep me sane.
 I never want to put you through so much unnecessary pain.
I've been through so much I don't know why.
But, I am strong, so strong I can bend the sky.
God is good and so are you.
You both have blessed me to see things through.
Thank you my child, my angel from above.
You've kept me breathing with your unconditional love.

Away

Today, when I saw you walk away,
I could sense it was over on this very day.
I knew that things would turn out this way.
I knew that your" love" would never stay.
Yet, still your game you attempted to play
made my soul feel special in every way.
However, time was past due even when we last lay
and we kissed and made love as I hoped and prayed.
What I must feel on this given day.
What heartache, what pain, what total waste. What was in
my heart was to yell out hey,
don't leave me now, please will you stay?
Unfortunately it was give and take, I gave my love to you,
and you took yours away.
So,why carry on or why try to make, something from
nothing, this was my mistake.
I'm always driving someone away
and I've met you as well, but still the same case.
So, farewell my love is all I must say.
May you continue to be sweet throughout your day.
May the happiness we shared always portray,
the love I had and the joy you gave,
if never again I get the chance to say
remember I love you always, in every way.

Love, or Is It?

I'm at a lost don't know where to turn.
My heart aches this terrible burn.
I want to run but I want to stay,
To give our love another day.
You have changed a lot or now I see.
That your love is painful or very tricky.
You accuse me of ways that are not of me.
And your accusations has made me into someone for all to see.
The sweet little, innocent, bubbly, country girl you once knew has been lost for awhile and don't know what to do.
She's a woman now, but not who she wants to be. You want me to be one way and my heart another.
I can no longer be undercover.
I cry a lot and hold stuff in because one day I hope one day not to cause a sin.
Please come back or leave me be. Just know my love for you, will be an eternity.

Have I Ever Told You I Love You?

Have I ever told you I love you or how much you mean to me?
When we're alone together with happiness and my love for you feels free.
Free to connect all the stars. Free to hold you close forevermore. Free to reach out when you're afar.
Have I ever told you I love you or how close I want you near? Because when you're not here, the love is gone, and therefore, I shed many tears.
Tears of joy that I met you.
Tears of pain because you're away.
Tears of fulfillment you brought into my life.
And tears of hope when I pray that you're here to stay.
If I never told you I love you Then, to you I apologize deeply.
But I do love you, My forever love
and I will love you; today, tomorrow, and for eternity.

I Never Understand

I never understand why people hurt the ones they love on
purpose
but I understand why purposely they get hurt by them.
(revenge)
I never understand why people hate on their friends or
strangers
but I understand why they were hated.
(jealousy-envy)
I never understand why women would stay in an abusive
relationship
but, I understand being in love can at times be
(abusive).
I never understand why a person would degrade
themselves for money,
but, I understand the need to
(survive).
One day when I understand,
I will be fully understood.

True Story

When I would tell you it's over
and that we're better off as friends.
You would tell me "no, it's not".
And that you don't want things to end.
Then I told you what I expected
before our relationship began.
And you told me you wanted this to work
and that you truly understand
If I ever asked were there others,
you'd reply "it's only me".
You'd tell me I have nothing to worry about,
not anything or anybody.
When I would ask are you sure of what you want,
your answer was that you're very certain.
Now I find myself heart broken once more
a victim of the same old game again.
As I would tell you how I feel
your response was "I feel the same".
While knowing in your heart from day one,
it was just a game.
Now you're manipulating someone else
and she's too blind to see.
But who am I to judge; yes she's blind
but, no different than me.

Torn Between The Two

Torn between the two, the old and the new. The old brings familiarity, a lot of chances, forgiveness, and a security blanket. The new bring promises that may be broken, the excitement of being desired, the getting to know each other phase.
Being a good person has its ups and down but can be very boring.
Being torn between the two brings out things in you that you may never knew existed.
Being torn between the two is scary, exciting, hot, invigorating and impulsive, but when it comes down to it. Don't act on impulse and don't set yourself up to be torn. Unless you are ready to move on to the next; you shouldn't take that chance.
Don't stray from the old because it's hard to get back in the fold.

Why I Love You So Much

Tell me once more
why I love so much
could it possibly be you laughter,
or is it your sweet, tender touch?
Do I love you for the way you talk
and speak so gently to me?
Or do I love you for your thoughts
and the way you express them lovingly?
Maybe it's your concern
and your pure honesty.
It's possible that I may love you
simply because you love me.
Do I love you for the kisses
and the massages at my ear?
Or maybe the indulging embrace
When you hold me so near.
Or maybe it's the soft caress
and the soothing and such.
Tell me once more
why I love you so much.

Why???

Why pretend to want to please me, to only end minutes later and while
you have been pleased , I'm left hanging and longing to please myself.
Why tell me you will give me everything but can afford nothing.
Why hold me close and whisper in my ear sweet love words, only to
fall asleep and have me aching for more.
Why say you love me when your actions say that you hate me.
Why promise to raise a family with me only to leave me while I'm still carrying our child.
Why pretend you want me only to push me away.
Why pretend to be a man when we both know you are still a child.
Why, Why, Why.

Truth

Thinking of you more and more,
I realize that you're not here.
Each time I attempt to reach out and touch you,
I'm saddened because you're nowhere near.
The longing for your touch
has grown twice as much as before.
The desire to feel you inside of me,
I will long forevermore.
When will situations get better?
I continue to question myself.
Or is there even any hope
for whatever we may have left?
I see us getting worse,
no matter how hard I try.
It takes us both to work it out.
Us means you and me, not just I.
Time will tell when it's over,
for time has never ceased to lie.
From this time I'll determine what is true;
the you love me's or goodbye.

Looking at You

Looking at you I see me. Even though it took me awhile to see myself.
Looking at you I see happiness. Even though it took me awhile to find my happiness.
Looking at you I see love. Even though it took me a while to love myself.
Looking at you, I see a family. Even though it took me awhile to realize that I already have one.
Looking at you I see beauty.
Even though I'm still searching for mine.
Here's to looking at you.

I Hate to See You Leave

I hate to see you leave
but it's probably the best thing.
When you came into my life
I proudly took you under my wing.
I did things for you I never did for another;
Not my mother, nor my father, my sister, or my brother.
I hate to see you leave,
but I think you'd better go.
It's so hard saying goodbye,
but this love will never grow.
We've had enough time
to try and make it right.
But now after all this time
I've finally seen the light.
I hate to see you leave,
but it's something you must do.
And no matter what happen from this day on
just remember, I'll always love you.

Creation

With the help of love, I've created someone to love
With the help of friend, I've created a life
With the help of my husband, I've created a legacy
With the help of God, I've created a family
With the help of all of this we created
YOU!!!

You

I want to give up on everything
all because of you.
Nothing matters in my life
except this love I hold so true.
I will give it all up
if it means I can have you.
Because your love is all I need
in my life to make it through.
I fell in love with you in the beginning.
Yet, I still love you in the end.
You are all that truly matters to me.
In your world, is my life I wish to spend.
Why must I feel this way for you?
The answer is yet to be proclaimed. Your love is all I've set
out for.
Your love is all I hope to gain. So, I ask you for some
closure
of this distance we have apart. But I ask for you, more than
anything because I love you with all my heart.

Which You Have

Being a father means being there when you're needed which, you have Being a father means loving and caring for all you loved ones
Which, you have Being a father means being there to lift me up when I am down which, you have. Being a father means being you
Which, you have. Thanks for being a father Thanks for being a man Thanks for being you. Happy Father's Day

Incomplete

My body aches for your touch,
but I cannot tell you.
My heartaches for your love,
but I cannot show.
My soul aches for you
more than you'll ever know.
My life aches
for your love to grow.

My thoughts linger for you
in my head
My pulse beats for you
at my feet.
My most cherished moments for you
are stored in my heart
but without you,
my whole life is incomplete.

My Best Friend

I see you in the morning.
I see you at night.
You are always there for me what a joyful delight.
You held me close and kept me warm,
through all those scary thunderstorms.
You chased away the monster
and made the boogey man leave.
I'm glad you're my father, and with your love I can achieve.
You taught me how to read, you taught me how to write,
you even remember my special bed time light.
So, on this day that comes once a year.
I'd like to say you're my best friend
far and near.
Happy Father's Day.

"Xo's" lullaby

Tell me how you like it and I'll do just what you like.
If it's wrong tell me the first time and the next time I'll do it right.
Whether, I start out much too slow or I finish much too fast.
As you point it out to me this time will surely out do the last.
There will be no need for corrections because I'll eventually get it right.
From then on, it shall be pleasant, as I read your lullaby goodnight.

I

I don't know how and I don't know why that I am never satisfied.
I see and want that, I see and want this and still my happiness doesn't exist.
Love is here then it's gone, will I ever have a place that I can call home?
I was with him, now I'm me, hoping one day that I can have a we.
I had it once, but it slipped away.
No more love was there, so I couldn't stay.
So, now I'm free and searching for me.
Hoping and praying to find myself and find a place where I belong.

Look Deeper

Your eyes are to young to see.
Your brain has not yet experienced enough to perceive.
Your heart refuses to embrace.
What we see upon your face.
We do not, could not, and shall not hate.
Just some of your chooses will someday seal your fate.
Some were bad and some were good
but, you should have understood that whether you're there
for us we were and will be there for you.
Didn't your father show and prove.
How many more stabbings can he take.
From the son that thinks he is fake.
We want you to do things for yourself.
No matter who you are you will always need a hand.
To get to the master plan.
So, never ever bite the hand that feeds you
for you never know who God has placed in you face.
To help you in this time and place.

Times.......Oh Times

These are the times when I feel so lonely
Like, I have no one but me.
There are times my life feels empty,
As though it will never be complete.
There are the times I dread the most
Because, it hurts so much inside.
These are the times I want life to end.
Only for reasons I can't describe.
There are times when I often cry
But, have no shoulders of which to lean.
There are times I often wonder.
What is actually my purpose of being.
These are the times I question myself
Of, when on me the sun will shine?
These are the times I come to realize that these are the times.....ooh these are the times!!!

No One Ever Knows

No one ever knows, what a person is thinking, so ask. No one ever knows, what a person is doing, so ask. No one ever knows, what a person is going through, so ask. Keep asking and go through it with them. No one ever knows if your last insult maybe the one that pushes that last nerve, so be kind. No one ever knows if that smile may brighten up their day. They may be afraid of what you may say, think, do, or feel. So, since they don't know and no one ever knows just be there until they do.

Broken Heart

I'm still shaking from the words you say. My tears can't hold back another day.
You were the 2nd person that's suppose to keep me safe.
Your words has also mentioned that I was a waste.
Your words were like daggers to my soul.
My heart bleeds deep and is filled with pain.
I doubt if we ever see her again.
Who am I now? Who have I become?
My soul is transitioning will I remain as one?
Someone new has come to the front now we both have to see what's what.
I feel as if I've been at war.
My heart, my body, my soul can take no more.
Love sucks, it's not rainbows and unicorns all the time.
It's dark, demanding, draining, brutal, blinding,
And deceiving. Damn "Love" it doesn't exist.
The tears just build a wall of mist. Be careful what you wish for they always say. For to you it will come one day.
I wished, hoped, prayed, and schemed, but all it made me was very mean.

__Anything__

If I ever meant "anything"
it should not be hard to say.
For if I ever meant "anything"
things would not have turned out this way.
And if you ever cared "anything"
I have to wonder was it true.
Right now, I would still be there with you.
And if my feelings ever meant "anything" may you
forever hold them in your heart.
Because your feeling meant everything
yesterday, today, and tomorrow when we're apart
but if I ever meant "anything"
to you, it may just be a thing.
However, to me, you meant everything
and that changes for nothing, not for "ANYTHING"!!!

Light to Dark

I use to be a bright sun but now I'm an eclipse.
I use to have fun and enjoy those tasty lips.
That was the past, yet still in the present.
The love I had is lost in the desert.
I tried getting it back many times over,
but I grow weary pretending I'm rover.
What went wrong, why treat me this way.
You knew who I was with no games to play.
I had goals and plans that I put aside because you believe
in the fire I had inside.

My Way

Walk with me, talk with me,
tell me all that I wish to hear.
That you love me and want me
and you miss having me near.
Hold me close to your heart,
whisper sweetly in my ear.
Tell my how you longed for this moment
that we are both, once again here.
Touch me, massage me
nibble at my ear.
Tell me how you've longed for the kiss
and the cares that's so dear.
Sigh with me cry with me
together we'll shed many tears.
Tell me all that I wish to hear,
but be truthful and give me a reason
to forget me every fear.

Employee of the month

Lies you told and my actions has cost me my job.
Your reactions, plots, and schemes has hurt yourself.
When you became the Devils elf.
Others have seen the lies you would sale,
but decided to stay in their own little jail.
What made you this way we will never know,
but behind me you too were kicked out the door.
Overly dramatic you became that day,
which has left others speechless and me nothing to say.
A crime was committed, but I dare not dwell
Because, one day you will face your own living hell.
I've learned one thing from this that and another
that I can count on myself and apparently no other.
Enemies come and go, but family and friends stick around because they are the one that help keep my feet on God's solid ground.

Breaking Time

Time has finally passed and I am certainly moving on.
At one time we shared much love, but now all of that is gone.
I'm trying to start over and it's not a simple task. Because I can't forget, My Love, and everything we've shared in the past.
I remember all the pain and the heartache from before. Some things I've tried not to think of but I simply cannot ignore. Each moment will be cherished I can honestly promise you that. However, we must not continue any longer and that is a certain fact.
So we're both moving on and I wish you much happiness. May the next person you meet give you nothing but the best.
The time has finally come for us to say our final goodbyes. We're moving on with time and may we both have promising lives.

Hater in My Camp *

I never thought that it would be you,
of all the things that we've been through.
Your selfish heart has made you bitter.
One day you will need a sitter.
You say I'm mean, negative and a Bitch,
but all the years of your negative
words has turned me into this witch.
Powers I do not possess and love
no longer here rests.
I've tried to be there but you push me away.
Day after day we have nothing to say.
When will this end, this pain that I feel.
You scream and shout is this for real.

What's Inside

Tell me what it is that you've been holding back. Don't beat around the bush get to the point be exact. I never knew just what you felt
so, I'm asking you right now. All the lies and fake excuses, this time I will not allow. I want to know what's in your heart
and what you truly feel for me. Express everything inside of you
so, I will know---truthfully. I won't hate you for your feelings,
but I will love you even more. Because you've finally been honest with me, you've finally opened the door.

The Past, The Present, The Future

The past is finally clear to me
now I know what everything meant.
I understand your ways now more than ever,
about the past and how each moment was spent.
You used me in the beginning,
but I could never actually see
that each moment you broke my heart
was because you never cared for me.
You're all that matters now,
like you were all that mattered then.
You could never have been my lover
because you were never even my friend.
You spoke of the next person
and how they were out to hurt me;
while the whole time it was you
I should have watched more carefully.
The past is clear now,
more than it's ever been before.
I will never love any other;
I've lost all trust, forevermore.

Remembering

Alone once more I begin to reminisce
about how happy I used to be.
Then with a blink of an eye, a twinkle in time,
I recall what is now reality.
The pain, the misery, the hatred, and sorrow
will last not only today.
But will continue tomorrow in my moment of depression
just as any other day.
Where did it all go, I frequently wonder,
why was it all washed away?
The love, the happiness, the desire for one another
all gone, without delay.
I pray for good times to come back again
to this aching, lonely heart.
For so much between us had been fulfilled
but the most memorable; our breaking apart.

My Promise

You are all I have in the world
and no one can tell me other
You are all I love in this world;
my daughters, my son, and my mother.
Who loves you all more than me?
There will never be another
Who will give their all for your needs?
Just I, your only true lover.

I love you all the more than I love myself,
yet, I know it doesn't always show
I pray, my loved ones, that you'll forgive me,
because my heart, you'll never know.
I am truly grateful to be blessed with you
your presence allows me to grow.
The way I wish us, as a family, to be,
I pray will one day show,

Who gives more love to my family-
who gives more love than me?
Only I can give you this true love,
because I know what lives within me.
Forgive me once more, I beg of you,
I promise better things to thee.
I promise one day, show you all,
just how much you mean to me!

In Me

Tell me once more
why I even bother living.
Each step forward sends me backwards
never receiving but always giving.
Attempting to bring happiness to others
not once even complaining .
Yet always miserable inside
from my own pain and suffering.

If I could end it all now
with the count of 1-2-3.
I'd gladly end my life, immediately;
it's not like anyone would even miss me.
They'd be so caught up with themselves
to even notice when I'm gone
Forget them, that solution works for me,
it ends the pain of being alone.

Nothing I want ever matters
not now, nor has it ever.
Yet, I continue carrying on,
I continue to be so clever.
How I do it, I've no idea.
I just do, and keep on crying.
The time is now that I wish to give up.
The time is now I wish to quit trying.

One World

A world so cold, of which no one cares.
Everyone for themselves, everyone with just stares.
Ask them for help and you're bound to get swears.
Offer them advice, they respond, "Do You Dare?"
How do you live in a world do cold?
Where people love no one- not the young or the old;
where the honest truth has yet begun to mold,
about how love and respect is worth more than gold.
With these two things it's sure to unfold;
A more peaceful world than what we behold.
Unfortunately, this world is, of yet, to be told so,
we continue living in a world so cold.
in search of a better day
constantly wondering
if the lord will ever look my way.
It can't possibly continue
to be this way forever.
There has to be some light;
my life has to get better.

What will I do if ever it doesn't?
Is it God's will, that my life mustn't?
I wonder what he has in store for me.
What possibilities, what achievements,
what many opportunities?

The harder I search
the more disappointed I am
to find no better way,
just another jam. .

What About Feelings ?

What day do we share the feelings we care.
Or do you care if we share them at all?
I don't think you care about the feelings we share because if you cared, you wouldn't be gone at all. On Monday "it's one thing" and Tuesday "it's another". On Wednesday "it's something else" and Thursday " it's whatever". On Friday "it's I'll see you" but on Saturday, still no show. Then on Sunday "you're resting" from being on the go. So, what day do we share the feelings we care or do you care if we share them at all? There is no day to share the feelings we care, simply because you care about no feelings, at all!

Invisible Love

I wish to touch My love
who is invisible.
I wish to feel him here
next to me.
I wish only for the love
that I've longed.
Invisible one,
please come to me.
Saying goodbye to My Love,
who is invisible-
was much harder
than watching him leave.
Because once he turned
and walked away.
There began my heart,
once more to grieve.
So, if seen, "My Invisible Love"
I promise to hold you close to me.
And never let you slip away again
from that longing that is so deep.

Outside

Look deeper than the outside
You'll be surprised at what you might see.
Look deeper than the outside.
Witness a totally different side of me.
The outside is only a cover.
This cover hides what's really inside.
For if you can look past the outside
you'll see what's put out, but each time denied.
Don't think you know what's on the inside
because of what the outside shows.
Don't think you know what's on the inside
because you don't, only I know.
However, if you take time to see the inside
you'll see things you knew never thought were there.
And the inside is where it all takes place
The transforming of actions you could never bare.
So, if the outside is all you see you should look deeper in
the days to come.
For you know nothing of what you see because the outside
tells nothing to anyone.

Looking

I'm looking at you, looking at her and
it's tearing me apart
I'm looking at you, looking at her
and this pain is piercing my heart.
I'm looking at you, looking at her
and I can't imagine what to do.
I'm looking at you looking at her
wishing it was me who appealed to you.
You're probably looking at me, looking at him
not caring at all what I do.
You're probably looking at me looking at him
not knowing I wish It were with you.
You're probably looking at me, looking at him
saying "I'm glad it's no longer me"
You're probably looking at me, looking at him
never thinking of what I want to be.
But then I'm looking at you, looking at her;
holding on to only a dream
A dream of you and me, looking at each other,
feeling, wanting, and thinking the same thing.

Peaceful (For Grandma)

One year it's been since you've been gone
and the feeling has not yet set in.
That I've lost my grandmother, my mother,
my fishing partner, and my best friend.
I see you in my dreams
and it seems as though you're still here.
When I awake I wish to call you
to hear you laughing in my ear.
However, my phone does not reach Heaven.
So, I try once more to sleep
to gather all the dreams I can of you
and store them in my heart for keeps.
Not now or ever will you be forgotten
by an who ever knew you.
No one can ever replace you, Grandma;
Mrs. Nellie Mae Wheeler a.k.a. "Coot".
Your life was well worth living every day,
even down to your final suffering.
However, suffer no more, you've done enough.
You're now at peace, up in Heaven.
I just wanted to take this time to remind
you that you're gone, but not forgotten.
And to say that December 1st was a day of grieving ,
but, also one to rejoice and to brighten.
Forever shall you be missed
100 times as much as you've ever been loved.
Just remember to look down on me and smile
because I'm glad you're at peace up above.

My Solemn Prayer

The Lord is my Sheppard, I shall not won't
I give my life to thee.
I'm crying out, praying and pleading to Him;
Dear God, please set me free!
You are all I have left in this uncaring world,
I'm sorry it took so long to see.
Now that I know better, I beg you forgiveness;
Please Father, gladly accept me.
One life to live, yet also wasted,
please open your doors to me.
Too much time passed, and not enough gained.
Take me now, no longer leave me be.
A sinful past, now in search of repentance.
How do I get closer to You?
I need you now in my heart
due to fear of soon being through.
Realizing now Christ that you're a necessity
in order to carry on. Doubting you all the days in the past;
my life now, a result of my being wrong.
I pray, Dear Father, you forgive me now
for all the wrong that I've done.
The sinful life, I've experienced before,
I want no more, My Lord, I want it none.
So, find it in you, My Heavenly Father, to bless and glorify
me. For I realize now the life I've lived, which didn't
include the almighty He. Now ready to change, I give my
word. I promise, blasphemy no more you are the one true
father and life I need, please shine your light and open your
doors.

A Better Way

Take me out of this world,
I have no place here.
Look out for my mother and children,
the only loved ones I hold dear.
Let them know much I love them
and, for sure, how much I care
Most of all, let them know
I could live no longer, I couldn't bare.
I'm sure you put me here because I have a purpose,
but I wonder if it's even enough.
I can't take it any longer, it's hurts so bad;
living daily tends to be so tough.
So, forgive me lord for this wish I have
of soon being taken away.
Please accept me with open arms
and remember the prayers that I have prayed.
Bless my mother and my children;
let them know how much they're loved.
Give them all the riches I couldn't in life,
but give me peace up above.
I beg you Lord Jesus to take me away
so that I can hurt no more.
And allow me, for once, to be at ease, proving the
worthiness I have in store.

Misery

Misery is a ***********! I for one, can honestly say.
Because from experience, I feel misery each and every day.
I sleep it, I drink it and I cry so much pain-- once I think of
all the things I
have still yet to gain. No peace, no happiness, no joy none
at all. Just misery comes in all figures, all fashions, and all
forms. I plan to destroy this feeling as soon as I possibly
can. Because misery is not a good feeling. I know from
experience,
I know firsthand.

Come Back To Me

Come back to me is all I ask of you. Let's recapture the moments we shared.
Come back to me is all I ask of you. Let's recall just how much we cared.
Come back to me is all I ask of you. Let's retry what we tried before.
Come back to me is all I ask of you. Let's make it right forevermore.
Come back to me is all I ask you. Let's try once more to succeed.
Come back to me is all I ask of you. Just come back because you're all that I need.

What Do I Do

What do I do now,
seeing that all the love is gone?
You used and abused my love
and then you left me all alone.
No reason why you ever did it,
not even an apology.
Just all the emptiness I felt
when you walked out on me.
I will cherish that love always
because I saved it just for.
And I will never love another
because that love is now gone, too.
When I speak of these feelings,
it's nothing more than true.
Now that you've taken it away,
I question myself
"What Do I do?"

Mistaken Identity

Who is this stranger before me?
You're not the same person I first met.
The personality in you now is totally different,
which leads me to have deep regrets.
I never imagined I'd speak this of the one I love
I never imagined this to be true.
I never imagined that a you would change as you did.
I never imagined that you'd hurt me, too.
Reality has struck and I see you
for the person that you really are.
I wish I had known this all before,
then I wouldn't have taken it this far.
I wouldn't have loved you for who I thought you were
or for whom I assumed you to be.
I would never have forsaken all others
as I have done disgracefully.
You've shown your true identity,
I have no choice, but to accept that. However, mistaken
as it may be, I'm convinced that it wasn't all an act.

<u>Going On</u>

I have never given up on love,
because there is no love to be found.
I have searched here and there,
far and wide, and all around.
There is no love for me, so my search is at an end.
There is no partner or confident, not a lover, or a friend.
I accept this fully and completely, without any disregards.
Even though these are the times
when accepting it is much hard.
I will go on as I have done for awhile
or quite some time- living on all the love I need;
that of God and that of mine.

This Love

If I could give this love I have for you
to someone who really needs it.
I'm sure I will begin to see
how it feels to be appreciated.
When it was given to you, it wasn't respected,
you trampled all over this love.
No matter what I did or how hard I tried
it never appeared as enough.
So, I'm giving this love to someone who needs it.
It no longer belongs to you.
All the pain and tears of being rejected with this love
are at the beginning of being through.
Don't waste your time such as I have done
for you'll never receive this love again.
I vow to spread this love to those who need it, but with you
it is at an end. Don't fret "My Dear" over this love it was
never what you wanted. "I don't love her, she's not
important"
was all you ever taunted. So, don't pretend this love was
ever valuable; to you it never meant a thing. To me this
love it was all that mattered, but lonely hearts will now
enjoy this love I bring.

Imagination

I'm calling out to you, but getting no answer
I can't understand what's going on.
The louder I yell, the more silent it becomes.
What is it that I'm doing wrong?
As I call to you, I listen for your voice.
Yet, no response is to be heard.
I'm calling out to you, I know you're there.
Could you please just utter one word?
Wait! Now I hear your voice, but I don't see you.
Where has my true love gone?
There it is again, I hear it once more,
but I turn to realize that I am alone.
As I search for you, you're still unfound
maybe I'm looking in the wrong place.
When I hear you voice utter a sound
once more, I turn to find imagination
staring me in the face.

A New Beginning

In Christ Jesus I now believe
cause only He can set me free
one life, I have, belongs to Him.
Each day not faithful, makes chances slim.
To have his love and many blessings.
Comes first to me above all things.
There is nothing more than Jesus Christ
that I wish to have more in my life.
Take me lord as I am.
Accept me, please, as much as you can,
I'm not perfect, only me.
As you grasp myself , I will grasp thee.
In my heart I hold you near.
Attempting to eliminate my fears.
However difficult, I will try.
Knowing you are always by my side.
Don't turn me away, I need you now.
Before you lord, I gladly bow.
One step at a time is all I take.
Promises to you, I will not break.
Take me henceforth under your wing,
let me enjoy he pleasure of life
Christ has to bring.

Gone, but Not Forgotten (For Grandma)

Gone, but not forgotten are the words I have for you. You've been blessed with a better place, one so peaceful and one so new you're now free from all your worries and you were spared of all your pain .
Those constant days and nights of suffering, you shall never endure again you've taught me to be strong, so for you that's what I'll do. However, nothing can replace my one and only you. All the smiles   and words of encouragement forever shall be missed, but always will be cherished, long after I seal that final kiss. You were a wonderful mother and grandmother to the family you left behind. And you were a caring friend to all who knew you in a way that was ever so kind . So, to you, I say farewell as you complete your journey. You're now blessed with peace and purity as you join the almighty "He". You are gone, but not forgotten, I just want to let you know. You've allowed to rejoice and, in return, I ,must let you go.

Giving Heart

Back up, stay away, don't even touch me.
I wish to be left alone.
I realize now what you're all about
or at least what you have shown.
I'm always caring, concerned, loving, and giving,
not to mention trying to take up the slack.

But, what on earth have you done for me,
what have you given me in return?
Only heartache, pain, misery, and sorrow;
you would think by now that I've learned.
Unfortunately, you don't learn overnight,
meaning I'll continue to be ever so sweet.
One day that sweetness will come to an end
and I will get the peace that I seek.

There will be no more giving and it won't matter to me
because, I will have all that I need.
I will feel peace and joy and love myself,
and nothing at all for this world so full of greed.
So, use my heart while you can.
Eventually, it will ache no more.
But, one day soon, will be stronger than ever and the
worries of the world, then, I will ignore.

Please, No More

I wish I could take this love I have in my heart
and throw it all away.
I wish I could never, ever love again,
but this feeling is here to stay.
It hurts so much thinking of it.
Why can't I just let it go?
My heart needs a break from all this pain.
Yet, this world will never know.

Although I may look at you and smile,
however it doesn't mean a thing.
Because in my heart lives all the love,
yet, all the hurt this world could bring.
Unfortunately, no one will ever know.
No one cares, so I'll hold it in.
Why can't I throw love all away?
Why won't the pain come to an end?

Lost Soul

Heavy is my heart
because it's filled with so much pain.
Weak is my mind from being torn of so much strain.
Stronger gets the pain
as my heart beats day to day.
Weary is my soul, because I no longer wish to pray.

Give up is my solution,
but often wonder if it's right.
Am I making the right decision,
will I finally see the light?
These questions I consider carefully
before I clearly make up my mind.
These frustrations eating at me constantly,
bringing on thoughts of suicide.

There has to be a better way.
Unfortunately, I can't see what it is.
This thought I should eliminate, not just for myself, but also my kids. However, it seems so much easier to give up and to just quit. But I know I will live to regret it, and I will never ever forget.

I Hate What I Know

I know I must let go, but how? I know I have to let go, but when?
I know holding on is making it worse. I know letting go will be the end. I hate to think of letting go. I hate to think of any end. I hate to think of what will happen. I hate going through this once again. I know to you, it's been long gone. I know to you, it will never be. I know to you, happiness is a virtue. I know I wish it were with me. I hate to think so negatively. I hate to think of what is gone. I know I must let go, but how? I know I have to let go, but when? I know holding on is making it worse. I know I wish we'd never end!!!

Self-Judgment

Stop wasting your time trying to judge me, but get to know me instead. Talk to me, hold conversation, learn the deepest thoughts in my head. I am just like you. I have a heart, and inside, I have feeling , too. Just by looking at me you'll never know all the things that I too, go through. So, get the whole picture before drawing your own, you'll be surprised at the similarities. The likes and dislikes, or things in common of two opposite personalities. Possibly not much difference in you or me, maybe even no difference at all. But, who are you to pass judgment on me? That is certainly not your call. So, spend more time getting to know me and less making many judgments. You too, I'm sure have issues inside, but wish not to reveal them in the public.

?

I have little trust left, for I've trusted all out. What do I do, lord, what is my life about.

What do I do? My life is in ruins. I wonder, what now because I feel so threatened. There is no where to turn or no one to turn to. Someone please answer the question, " What do I do?". Each road twice taken tends to be a dead end. The crossroads where I stand, has only losses, no wins. I've tried for so long, yet, I feel so through. Someone please answer the question of "What do I do?" Trapped, is exactly where I am. Strapped down, caught completely in a jam. My body worn out of all the stress I ever knew. My soul ready to give in, yet I still wonder what to do. I have little hoe left, for I've hoped for so long, I have little faith left, for it too will soon be gone.

What's Next

Snow falling like my spirit, and it's just as cold as my heart.
Where did it go wrong? Who can reset my default?
The one I thought would love me forever and be there for me. Has abandoned my light and left me for dim.
Is that why I look so very grimm? I'm hoping to return to the beginning, where it all took place.
So, he can look at me and caress my lovely face.
I don't want to give up but he makes it so easy.
So, why am I the only one feeling so very queasy.?
Every little thing that he does makes me want to scream.
Oh lord even the way he eats that dang ice cream. I don't know what to do, I am so very lost.
So, I ask you my heavenly father, since you are the boss.

Reality of it All

There's one thing my life has missed all these years. It is a lack of religion. Going to church and believing in Christ, and then faith, I had none. All this time I've allowed to past without acknowledging Him. No wonder I'm having it so hard, no wonder my chances are so grim. Getting closer to God now is my main priority. That's something no one can change. If blessed just a little by my almighty father, my life I promise to rearrange. Once rearranged, I honestly vow to The Father , nothing but changes for the better. To go to church, pray, and I talk to him more, And to thank Him, my most important debtor. Looking at life from a different perspective, I'm realizing what has to be done. I need to turn to the lord, pray, and ask for forgiveness and hope that I am supposed to do, only then, will my job be done. And from this day on, my father will say, "my child, now your life has begun".

Lost

So many things floating through my head,
Yet, my mind is still confused.
Knowing my wants and needs in life,
but still unable to produce.
What must I do to be complete
when will this whirlwind end?
Where can I go for satisfaction
when will my joy begin?

I see no way that any pleasure
will ever come to me.
One life so lost, one life so wasted,
my life - so full of misery.
Lord, take this life away from me,
please give me something worth living,
allow me joy once, with a peaceful life,
in this flesh for which you have given.

It forever feels meaningless to carry on;
this flesh holds no purpose.
Why allow me to continue to endure this pain,
I'm sure it will certainly get worse.
I try to keep positive and think for the better,
but each time I'm again shut down.
Lord, please allow me something good from this life.
Lord, please will you issue my crown?

CPSIA information can be obtained
at www.ICGtesting.com
Printed in the USA
BVOW04s0828190317
478862BV00001B/28/P

9 781618 635020